EDUCATOR'S
QUICK REFERENCE GUIDE

to grit in the classroom

by Laila Y. Sanguras

WHAT IS GRIT?

GRIT is intense passion coupled with sustained perseverance (Duckworth, 2016). The order of those descriptors is important.

Grit = passion + sustained perseverance

What Is Passion?

We often forget the importance of passion in cultivating grit. Another way to conceive of passion is to consider the **"why"** of what we are asking of our students. This **"why"** goes beyond curriculum standards—it is individual and deeply personal. Consider anything you've ever done that has been difficult. You inevitably hit a metaphorical wall and had a moment to decide whether you would continue pushing forward or give up. If you decided to keep going, it was likely because your passion (your **"why"**) motivated you. The same is true for students.

What Is Perseverance?

Most of us understand the relationship between perseverance and success. Achievement, especially an elite level of achievement, does not happen without struggle. As we bring concepts to life for our students, we tell stories of authors, scientists, and political figures. These stories often center on the challenges faced and overcome, highlighting the greatness and esteem that accompanies "stick-to-itiveness." This we understand.

Cultivating Passion

Let's stop talking about passion as though it's something "found," and admit that it is the result of actions. It's cultivated, like a love of 18th-century art or an appreciation for fancy cheese. Curiosity leads to interest, which leads to passion. It's that simple.

Consider your weekly lesson plans. Where have you provided opportunities for students to become passionate? How much time are you dedicating to developing curiosity? We need to acknowledge that we are failing our students by not providing them with thousands and thousands of opportunities to be curious. We are failing them by sending them on their way with wishes of "taking the road less traveled" and encouraging them to "following their passion" and reminding them of "oh, the places you'll go." We mean well, but need to do more.

Building Perseverance

Opportunities to persevere stem from struggle. News outlets cover the most dramatic of stories, highlighting people who escape from difficult circumstances or survive illnesses. For most, perseverance is much more basic: It's sticking with something when we want to quit. Perseverance is a universal behavior that we all share regardless of age or station in life. We have all been on the precipice of struggle, but how we respond in that struggle can vary greatly.

If we want to build perseverance in our students, we must instill in them the belief that giving up is not an option. We need to strategically place them in difficult academic environments. We need to push them in every class, in every subject, every day.

3 STRATEGIES FOR INTRODUCING STUDENTS TO GRIT

1. **Introduce students to people who have demonstrated passion and perseverance in pursuit of their goals.** Depending on the abilities of your students, choose reading selections accordingly. Students can read biographies of J. K. Rowling or Angie Thomas in language arts, Marie Curie or Albert Einstein in science, Nelson Mandela or Abraham Lincoln in social studies, and Isaac Newton or Marjorie Lee Browne in mathematics. You could also select a number of other people, including Michael Jordan, Frida Kahlo, and Jay-Z. Most people who have "made it" in their fields have done so because of grit.

2. **Encourage students to recognize grit in themselves and those around them.** Ask them to journal about someone they know personally who exemplifies (or doesn't) the kind of passion and perseverance needed to be successful. When discussing current or historical events with your students, make sure "grit" is part of the conversation. Never miss a moment to bring grit to the forefront of your students' minds.

3. **Illustrate what grit does and doesn't look like.** When students understand what grit is all about, you can show them **Table 1**, which lists ways in which students may demonstrate grit and warning signs that they may not be demonstrating grit. Ask students to add specific behaviors and actions to the table so that they can apply what they've learned. By doing so, students can transfer their understanding to their own experiences.

Table 1
Student Demonstrations of Grit or Lack of Grit

Signs of Students Demonstrating Grittiness	Warning Signs of Students Without Grit
• They get a bad grade on a math test and ask you how they can do better next time. • You introduce a project, and your students get excited about the possibilities. • They can be overly chatty in group projects but typically on topics related to the assignment.	• They get huffy when they get a bad grade, throwing away their tests. • They are annoyed by the open-endedness of a project and just want you to tell them how to get a good grade. • They ask you for extra credit, often at the end of the grading period.

NOTE. Reprinted with permission from Sanguras, 2017.

ENCOURAGING STUDENTS TO SET SUPER STRETCH GOALS

SMART goals have made their way from elementary school students to Fortune 500 employees (Mind Tools, n.d.). An acronym to simplify the goal-setting process, SMART reminds us that goals should be specific, measurable, achievable, relevant, and time-bound. But where is the dream . . . the passion . . . the catapult toward success? It's completely missing, and this is where we need to step in to support our students.

Duckworth (2016) proposed that goals are built into a hierarchy with actions at the bottom and goals above, leading to a super, or stretch, goal. Look at **Figure 1**. The SMART goals are those under the stretch goal. They still fit the criteria of attainable goals, but each specific, measurable, achievable, relevant, and time-bound goal is directly linked to the ultimate "why," or the dream. And that is what makes the difference when trying to convince your students to do things they don't want to do.

> **"GRIT** is the ability to stay focused on that super goal, regardless of distractions and setbacks."

> **"SELF-CONTROL** is the ability to choose to complete the actions leading to that goal instead of choosing an activity that does not lead to the goal."

First, we have to help our students dream (and we should be dreaming alongside them). And then we help them identify the smaller goals that will get them closer to their dreams, followed by daily actions. This changes the game when it comes to identifying objectives for our students; it is no longer up to us to write concise, neat statements on the board identifying the reasons behind our lessons. Instead, the objectives are personalized and connected to each student's super stretch goal.

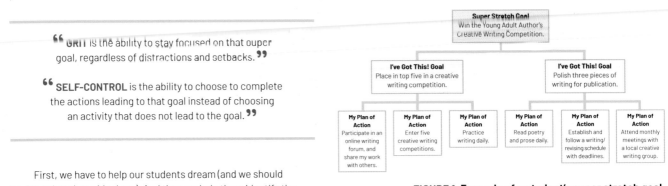

FIGURE 1. **Example of a student's super stretch goal. Adapted with permission from Sanguras, 2017.**

PURSUING EXCELLENCE THROUGH EFFORT

Duckworth and Gross (2014) proposed two equations to explain how talent leads to achievement:

$$\text{Talent} \times \text{Effort} = \text{Skill}$$

$$\text{Skill} \times \text{Effort} = \text{Achievement}$$

Notice that effort counts in both equations. In fact, you can rewrite the equations as:

$$\text{Talent} \times (\text{Effort} \times \text{Effort}) = \text{Achievement}$$

$$\text{Talent} \times \text{Effort}^2 = \text{Achievement}$$

Take a moment to consider the power of this path to achievement. Sure, talent is important, but effort is even more influential. That's pretty incredible.

Duckworth (2016) suggested that someone twice as talented who puts forth half the effort as another person may have the same level of skill as that person, but will achieve less over time.

When we place an emphasis on effort, authentic effort, with our students, we are also showing them a way to improve their performance. And by creating a community that values true effort, you are creating individuals who know how to take their skills, pursue their passions, and excel.

4 WAYS TO DEVELOP GRIT

Bloom (1985) outlined three stages of developing talent in children:

- The first stage is all about having fun, romancing the discipline, and receiving external rewards. These rewards, things like stickers and praise, come from teachers and parents and serve as encouragement to continue the pursuit of a student's interest. Interests at this stage can be broad or specific and change often.
- In the second stage, this interest becomes a part of the child's identity. She starts to describe herself as a soccer player or writer and finds intrinsic motivation for digging deeper into the discipline. Teachers continue to emphasize the fun and excitement in learning, while also having high expectations. Parents support their child by finding appropriate classes, tutors, coaches, etc.
- In the final stage, children find the larger meaning in their interests and work toward mastery. They love competition and enjoy the demands placed upon them. In finding a greater purpose, they identify careers that align with their interests. Teachers become mentors and share a similar passion for and commitment to the discipline. Parents support their children's pursuits and continue to find (and fund) outside support.

Duckworth (2016) identified four components of grit that support Bloom's (1985) theory. By understanding each of these, we can deconstruct what it means to build grit.

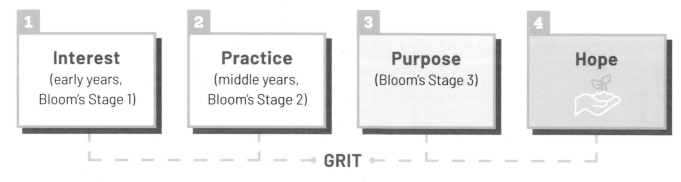

1	2	3	4
Interest (early years, Bloom's Stage 1)	**Practice** (middle years, Bloom's Stage 2)	**Purpose** (Bloom's Stage 3)	**Hope**

GRIT

4 WAYS TO DEVELOP GRIT, Continued.

1. Interest

Interest generally doesn't arrive like a flash of lightning or a pizza delivery. The interest that leads to passion is often the result of trying lots of different things. Part of the childlike discovery is finding out what you enjoy and where your talents lie. It doesn't matter if it's a lasting passion or meaningful or fruitful.

Mehta (2015) suggested that we design T-shaped curriculum. Essentially, the top part of the T symbolizes the breadth while the tail represents the depth:

- **Breadth** is where we add the bells and whistles—we use music, video clips, and interactive activities to engage our students and get them to take a bite out of what we're offering. This is when we really sell our content. It's surely fun, but isn't going to build fascination. It's akin to flying over a city—you may ooh and ah a couple of times, but you don't know enough to know what you want to know more of.
- **Depth** is when you "buzz the tower" with a fly-by. You get close enough to incite interest so that students begin generating questions about the content. We know that interest is personal, so we allow students to choose the towers they want to buzz. Worst case, teachers choose the areas for students to deepen their learning. The crucial part is to pay attention to the sparks so that they can be fanned later.

Passion begins with discovery. Duckworth (2016) suggested that children need to be exposed to "interest-stimulating experiences." Think about this in the context of your school and classroom. How many times are students' interests triggered in a calculated way?

2. Practice

To turn an interest into a passion, interest-triggering activities need to happen over and over again. The art of practice is placing yourself in opportunities so that you can feel this joy again and again. People who are gritty are never comfortable with what they've accomplished. They work daily to improve in their pursuit of excellence. They are also comfortable with their weaknesses and understand that they must attack these weaknesses in order to reach their goals (Duckworth, 2016). In addition to retriggering your interest through practice, you also must focus on improvement in order to reach your goals.

This kind of practice is rigorous and exhausting. So, although building your interest is fun, practicing takes a deep commitment to where you're going. It also takes a lot of time. So, if we are to promote this kind of practice in schools, we have to vertically align our interest-triggering activities. That means we have to take this interest-building business seriously, as seriously as we take our curriculum standards and standardized tests. How?

- We set the expectation that we will find our content interesting. Think of it like a self-fulfilling prophecy or an "If we build it, they will come" philosophy.
- We need to hold students accountable for building upon their prior interests. With technology today, it's easier than ever for students to create digital portfolios that can "travel" with them from year to year.

3. Purpose

Because persistence is such an integral part of grit, identifying a purpose is essential to maintaining focus. This purpose is what makes challenges bearable and is enough to sustain focus when you may want to give up. The purpose can be very specific (e.g., to improve the education of children) or more broad (e.g., to contribute to the research in my field). Purpose is developed from a lot of factors, many outside of school, but typically has a strong tie to passion.

4. Hope

Hope in the context of grit is different from the hope that comes with luck, just as it's one thing for a 16-year-old to say, "I hope my parents get me a new car," versus, "I hope my studying for that chemistry test pays off." One is a shot in the dark—the teenager has no reason to believe he will actually be getting a new car—while the other is a product of his practice.

Duckworth (2016) suggested that hope accompanies a feeling of power. If you feel in control of your success and where you're headed, you're more likely to feel hopeful than if it feels like a crapshoot. Hopeful people are optimistic. When they see that they are failing or not doing very well, they face their weaknesses and make a plan for improvement. But let's face it; you're a teacher. You already know what hope is, and it's likely the only thing that gets you out of bed some mornings. You believe in yourself and in your students that you can do better than yesterday.

 Educator's Quick Reference Guide to Grit in the Classroom © Prufrock Press Inc.

BALANCING IDENTITY AND GRIT

Teachers need to accept that they play a crucial role in helping all of our students establish their identities. We want a thousand things for our students, right? But to narrow those down, we want them to believe in their abilities, to know that they are worth more than a singular success or failure, and that with grit they can overcome obstacles. Those beliefs, not their labels, should be at the core of students' identities.

Labels are important for really one reason: They allow us to identify what our students need and how we can support them. But the importance of identity development sometimes gets lost in our mission to appropriately assign labels to the students who need them (i.e., gifted, special education, ADHD, etc.). Because of this reason, we cannot allow a child's label to create the parameters of our expectations for that child.

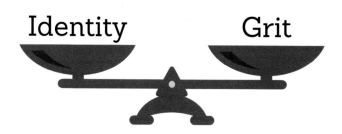

2 TIPS FOR A GRITTY CLASSROOM

1. Make "hard" the norm.

Students at all levels need to be challenged daily and in every subject. As experts in our field, we should provide scaffolding and support to those who need it, but no longer will we hear our students whine about having to work hard as if it's out of the ordinary, because it isn't. They will still complain, because that's part of their job description, but their complaints will be focused elsewhere.

2. Help students identify their talents and strengths in every domain.

Then, encourage and push them to strive toward excellence in those areas. Maybe Janie really struggles in math, but for some bizarre reason has the Pythagorean theorem memorized. She can even explain it to the most novice students in a way that you never could. Well, every time that theorem comes up, Janie is your expert and takes over the class to explain it. Is this "talent" going to change Janie's life? Probably not. But it will give her authentic confidence and open doors to new theorems she might find interesting. That's a win.

In the bigger picture, we want Janie to understand where her true strengths lie. Sure, she's got the Pythagorean theorem in math, but that doesn't make her feel alive like writing poetry. Or playing softball. Or debating. Or singing. You get the picture. Depending on the development of your students, strengths may be viewed as interests. For example, Antonio may not be a great actor, but he loves being onstage and spends all of his free time running lines. If we want to help our students perform at elite levels, we need to recognize their strengths.

IT'S COOL TO BE PASSIONATE

Newport (2012) suggested that people who enjoy their jobs, who in turn describe themselves as being passionate about their careers, are afforded competence, respect, autonomy, creativity, and sense of impact. Their "passion" comes from experiencing each of these regularly and authentically. So let's talk about how these attributes can be emphasized in your classes.

Do you remember Vygotsky's Zone of Proximal Development (as cited in Daniels, 2005)? Consider this zone as you design your lessons and focus on developing competency of each lesson's objective.

> ### Quick Review
>
> Vygotsky's Zone of Proximal Development is what we now think of as scaffolding (Daniels, 2005). You design learning experiences just beyond what a student can do alone, but provide the support necessary to achieve success. The zone continues to move as the child's skills develop.

2 STRATEGIES FOR DEVELOPING GRITTY LESSONS

1

Determine what your students know. You can do this by having students describe what they know about a topic, or you can give them a more formal preassessment. This process should be focused on the main objective of the lesson, not on the details. Essentially, consider what you want your students to remember about the lesson 10 years from now—that should be at the center of your assessment of what they know.

2

Create learning experiences designed to lead your students to feeling competent. This doesn't mean that you hand out a trophy when your students master the objective or that you dilute your content; it just means making room for all students to be and feel competent in your classroom.

CREATING A CULTURE OF RESPECT AND CREATIVITY

Creating a culture of respect begins on the first day of class. You need to show that you value your students and their opinions. You respect them as human beings and accept that they may not love your class or your content or you as much as you would like.

We must also create classrooms for our students that center on *autonomy*, *responsibility*, and *self-control*. When we are given autonomy and respect, we have the freedom to be creative. We can come up with new ways to solve problems and new problems to solve. So just by making small adjustments in your classroom's balance of power, you are already providing your students with the space needed to be creative.

You can kindle the passion of your students by helping them see that their actions and their learning matter. Authentic assessments begin with an essential question—these questions provide the guiding purpose for your lessons, and they get to the significance. Even though you're teaching a lesson on fractions, you're actually helping students understand how many parts create a whole and that each part is important. It's not a big leap to understanding that students are those parts that create your whole classroom/school/team. Ultimately the authentic assessment, the culminating activity, should be engaging and directly tied to the essential question.

By designing authentic learning experiences for your students, you are providing them with the path between the ***"Why do we have to know this?"*** and the ***"Ah, I get it now"*** moments.

GETTING PARENTS ON BOARD

Grit cannot be cultivated in an environment where children are given everything they want. It also can't be developed if they never get a taste of earned success. Grit can be strategically developed through failure and healthy responses. The most efficient way to do this is by combining efforts between school and home, building a roadmap headed toward success.

Talking to Parents About Grit

Commitment

A person cannot develop grit without commitment. Encourage the parents of your students to talk with their children about their own commitments and the struggles they've faced when honoring them. As part of the learning/teaching process about what it means to be gritty, encourage your students' parents to talk with their kids about times they wanted to quit something and didn't, or a time they did quit and how that felt. Parents often feel that they have to set the perfect example for their children, but because grit can be so messy and painful to develop, kids are better off if they have a sense of what this looks like in reality. They also need to understand that even adults experience the same feelings they do.

Struggle

You can help parents understand that, although building grit is essential to raising independent and successful adults, it's hard. As a teacher, you design learning experiences to challenge your students and you scaffold those assignments to allow the students to be successful. But when a kid is 7 and wants to go to recess, or 13 and wants to talk to her friends, or 17 and has to go to work, she doesn't want to work hard. She wants to move on with "good enough" effort that really is far from good enough. Prepare your parents for this. Tell them that their child will struggle, but that it's worth it. Tell them that their child will want to quit, but you'll be there every step of the way. Parents need to understand that this is coming so they can prepare themselves and can support their children at home.

Praise

It's also helpful to discuss how parents should praise their children, focusing on the process of learning, struggling, and persevering. Although it's easy to celebrate the A or the first-place trophy, we all need to remember to emphasize the importance of the journey. You can model for parents how they can talk with their child about how it felt to work hard, encouraging them so that they use similar language when preparing for the next challenge.

Success

3 TIPS FOR A GRITTY SCHOOL CULTURE

Communication of the kind of culture, and what grit means, is essential to building and maintaining a gritty school culture:

1
Ensure that everyone at every level understands that your school is a place where people go for it, where no one holds back and no one gives up.

2
Encourage students to talk about their "epic fails" and (I love this one) to view failures as data (Ricci, 2015).

3
Set and communicate expectations.

YET

Understanding grit provides the context we need to understand why both rigor and passion are so important to include in our curriculum. Yet, you've got this. Knowing what you now know about the implications of persistent effort, you can begin to think about how you can provide regular opportunities for your students to struggle their way through problems.

You know the importance of a gritty school culture, of building the capacity for a school full of people (and their parents) to support each other as they strive for excellence. You understand how grit aligns with our prior understanding of mindsets and learning orientations.

> Grit is not the solution to the issues you may be experiencing in the classroom; it is one way to conceive of the effort and skill needed to achieve at high levels.

You have practical ideas for nurturing curiosity as if it were a standard of our curriculum. Most of all, you are invigorated and inspired to go to the next level, to set and pursue your stretch goals, and to be the absolute best for every student every day.

References

Bloom, B. S. (1985). *Developing talent in young people.* New York, NY: Ballantine Books.

Daniels, H. (Ed.). (2005). *An introduction to Vygotsky.* New York, NY: Psychology Press.

Duckworth, A. (2016). *Grit: The power of passion and perseverance.* New York, NY: Scribner.

Duckworth, A. L., & Gross, J. J. (2014). Self-control and grit: Related but separable determinants of success. *Current Directions in Psychological Science, 23,* 319–325.

Mehta, J. (2015). *Breadth and depth: Can we have it both ways?* [Web log post]. Retrieved from http://blogs.edweek.org/edweek/learning_deeply/2015/07/breadth_and_depth_can_we_have_it_both_ways.html

Mind Tools. (n.d.). *SMART goals: How to make your goals achievable.* Retrieved from https://www.mindtools.com/pages/article/smart-goals.htm

Newport, C. (2012). Why 'follow your passion' is bad advice. *CNN.* Retrieved from http://edition.cnn.com/2012/08/29/opinion/passion-career-cal-newport

Ricci, M. C. (2015). *Ready-to-use resources for mindsets in the classroom: Everything educators need for building growth mindset learning communities.* Waco, TX: Prufrock Press.

Sanguras, L. Y. (2017). *Grit in the classroom: Building perseverance for excellence in today's students.* Waco, TX: Prufrock Press.

About the Author

Laila Y. Sanguras is a former middle school teacher. Her interest in grit stemmed from observing her students balk at challenging activities in school, yet excel despite struggling in areas outside of school. She received her doctorate in educational psychology from the University of North Texas.

$12.95 US

PRUFROCK PRESS INC.™

Copyright ©2018, Prufrock Press Inc.

Edited by Katy McDowall

Layout design by Allegra Denbo

No part of this guide may be reproduced without written permission from the publisher. Visit https://www.prufrock.com/permissions.aspx.

Please visit our website at https://www.prufrock.com.

Printed in the USA

ISBN-13: 978-1-61821-790-5

51295

9 781618 217905